PETER HAISLER

How to write
a good research paper

Samfunds
litteratur

Peter Haisler
How to wirte a good research paper

1. udgave 2011
© Samfundslitteratur 2011

OMSLAG Annette Borsbøl, Imperiet
LAYOUT SL grafik
SATS SL grafik, Frederiksberg (www.slgrafik.dk)
TRYK Narayana Press, Gylling (www.narayana.dk)
ISBN 978-87-593-1555-2

Samfundslitteratur
Rosenørns Allé 9
1970 Frederiksberg C
Tlf.: 3815 3880
Fax: 3535 7822
slforlagene@samfundslitteratur.dk
www. samfundslitteratur.dk

Alle rettigheder forbeholdes. Kopiering fra denne bog må kun finde sted på institutioner, der har indgået aftale med COPY-DAN, og kun inden for de i aftalen nævnte rammer.Undtaget herfra er korte uddrag til anmeldelse.

INDHOLD

Foreword   7

Chapter 1 Introduction   9
    The website and other useful resources   10

Part 1. Before   11

Chapter 2 Some generic advice   13
    Everything is allowed   13
    Start the project process early   13
    Start collecting information early   13
    Go straight to those who have the most relevant knowledge   14
    Start the writing process early   14
    Be critical   15
    Keep it simple   15

Chapter 3 Forming a project group   16
    Align your expectations   16
    Make rules   17
    Final advice   18

Chapter 4 Your supervisor   19
    Choosing your supervisor   20
    Make it easy for your supervisor   20
    Prior to each meeting with your supervisor   21
    Meeting your supervisor   21
    What students expect from their supervisor   22

Part 2. During   23

Chapter 5 Choosing a Research Question (RQ)   25
    Different types of RQs   25
    How to find a relevant RQ   26

Brainstorm	27
Three criteria for choosing your RQ	28
Choosing your analytical perspective	28
Choosing the specific topic (of analysis)	29
Formulating your RQ	30
When you have settled on a RQ	32
Final advice	32

Chapter 6 Forming assumptions, sub-questions, and hypotheses — 34

Assumptions	34
Sub-questions	34
Hypotheses	35
Choose the hypotheses with the greatest explanatory power	36
Final advice	36

Chapter 7 Planning the research process — 38

A typical research paper	38
Final advice	39

Chapter 8 The introduction — 40

Chapter 9 Methodology — 41

What is methodology?	41
Why methodology?	41
The contents of the methodology chapter	42
The philosophy of science (including epistemology and ontology)	42
The overall methodological approach (i.e., inductive or deductive)	43
The delimitations (i.e., your methodological choices)	44
The empirical data (qualitative and/or quantitative data)	45
Choice of theories (including critique)	46
Structure of the research paper	46
Validity and reliability	46
The literature review	48
Definition of key terms	48
Final advice	48

Chapter 10 Using empirical data — 50

Qualitative and quantitative data	50

Final advice	51
Chapter 11 Choosing and using theories	**52**
What is a theory?	52
Critiquing theories	54
Examples of theoretical critiques	55
How to employ theories	55
Use different theories to answer the same RQ	56
Chapter 12 Analysis	**57**
Final advice	57
Chapter 13 The conclusion	**59**
Final advice	60
Chapter 14 Future perspective	**61**
Chapter 15 Executive summary	**62**
Chapter 16 Layout and language	**63**
The layout	63
The language	64
Quotation, plagiarism, and referencing	64
Final advice	65
Chapter 17 Key elements in a good research paper	**66**
Final advice	66

Part 3. After 69

Chapter 18 Oral examinations	**71**
Preparing your presentation	71
Generic questions at the oral exam	72
Final advice	73
Chapter 19 The grading elements – the examiner's manual	**74**

Chapter 20 Feedback after the examination					76

Useful books					77

About the author					79

FOREWORD

Almost ten years of teaching methodology and philosophy of science at Copenhagen Business School and the University of Copenhagen has convinced me of the need for a short, practical book about how to construct and write a good academic research paper.

Although many similar books have been written, it is my experience that students do not read them (they are often very long); hence, this short practical book.

The book is based on my experiences as a lecturer in the methodology and philosophy of science, as a supervisor and examiner, as well as numerous interviews with other examiners, censors, teachers, and students. I would like to thank all the supervisors, teachers, censors, and students from whom I have received invaluable feedback on and input to this book. Especially, I would like to thank Katherine Greenberg for her many comments and ideas.

Peter Haisler
Copenhagen, April 6, 2011

CHAPTER 1
INTRODUCTION

This concise book gives tangible advice on how to write a good academic research paper. It is useful for those writing term papers, one-year projects, bachelor's or master's theses. The book is structured chronologically in accordance with the research and writing process and is thus divided into three parts: *Before*, *During*, and *After*.

The learning objectives of most study programs at tertiary educational programs are almost entirely based on methodological criteria. This means that all academic research papers – short as well as long – are largely graded according to the quality of their research methodology. Thus, if you want to obtain a good grade on your academic research paper, you need to have a solid understanding of both the various existing research methodologies and how to structure an academic paper around them. The latter is the focus of this book.

In short, methodology is about making *choices*. A student writing an academic research paper is constantly making methodological choices, either implicitly or explicitly. This book aims at qualifying these choices and to enable the reader to make appropriate methodological choices, and critically evaluate the consequences.

In short the book offers:

- A quick overview of how to write an academic research paper.
- Ways to organize the process of writing an academic research paper.
- An overview of the most common problems encountered when writing academic research papers.
- Practical guidelines that can be used throughout the writing process and during the examination.
- An understanding of some of the different research methodologies.
- Advice on how to obtain good grades on exams.

THE WEBSITE AND OTHER USEFUL RESOURCES

The aim of this book is to give you the basic insights into how to write a good academic research paper. If you want to go into more depth regarding the various topics you may consult the chapter on useful books. Here you will find references to a number of the best books available on the various topics.

Furthermore, the book is supported by the website www.researchpaper.samfundslitteratur.dk. Here, you can find a range of potential research topics appropriate for short and long research papers. You can also find several examples illustrating and further explaining the topics in this book, including examples of research questions, analyses, theories, introductions, methodology chapters, etc., all taken from authentic research papers. These examples are intended to provide the inspiration and skills you need to write a good academic research paper.

PART 1
BEFORE

This first section deals with the topics you have to consider before starting the actual writing process. This includes initial advice on the working process as well as advice on how to benefit from working in a group and how to use your supervisor.

CHAPTER 2
SOME GENERIC ADVICE

EVERYTHING IS ALLOWED

When I supervise students, they frequently ask whether their methodological choices are 'okay,' or which of their choices I believe is the best. My answer is always the same: that they should do what they believe is best. As long as they can provide reasonable arguments for their methodological choices, (almost) everything is allowed. Methodology is essentially about making the *best choices* in order to answer your research question (RQ), taking into account the resources you have at your disposal. There is no *one right way* to construct a research paper, not least because all RQs are different. Consequently, I always recommend that my students structure their research papers in the way that provides the most logical answer to *their* specific RQs. So, 'everything is allowed' as long as you can justify your methodological choices with good arguments.

START THE PROJECT PROCESS EARLY

Do not underestimate how long it takes to write a research paper. Often, you will arrive at a more realistic estimate by taking your initial estimate and multiplying it by a factor of three. In particular, if you are working in a group, you can expect that the many discussions required will often take much longer than you anticipate; therefore, start the process as soon as possible.

START COLLECTING INFORMATION EARLY

Identifying, collecting, and reading information is time-consuming. In addition, you have to compete with others for the same limited number of books and articles. As a consequence, the books and articles you order from the library will frequently only be available after three to four months. Furthermore, if you want to conduct interviews, make sure to identify and contact the relevant experts as soon as possible. Likewise, if you have to write about an organization in your research paper, it is important that you initiate contact early.

GO STRAIGHT TO THOSE WHO HAVE THE MOST RELEVANT KNOWLEDGE

When looking for information, try to interview experts from universities, government ministries, the media, at NGOs, or wherever experts in your field may be. Interviews give you valuable first-hand expert knowledge and demonstrate that you are able to take action independently. Interviews also give you a head start, because experts can lead you in the right direction, tell you where to find the right information, and highlight what the key problems are in relation to your RQ. Most experts are willing to spend fifteen to twenty minutes answering your questions, and most experts love to talk about their field of expertise. Just remember to be well prepared for the interview.

START THE WRITING PROCESS EARLY

Whether you work alone or in a group make sure to start the writing process early. Writing your thoughts down on paper forces you to think about the words, formulations, and topic, making it far more concrete and thus easier to discuss. Groups may talk for weeks and weeks, believing that they have a common understanding on what their research paper is going to look like. This is hardly ever the case. Starting the actual writing process too late may cause considerable problems because people have different writing styles. These problems can start out as different opinions on how to get the work done but then turn into personal conflicts between group members. Quite often groups split up one to three weeks before they have to hand in their research paper because they started the writing process too late and only at the last minute realized that they could not work together. Their grades are often affected quite negatively.

BE CRITICAL

When writing a research paper, always be critical of the empirical data, the theories, the 'experts,' and last, but not least, of your own subjective assumptions.

KEEP IT SIMPLE

Keep your RQ and your research paper simple. Remember every now and then to go back to basics and ask yourself: What is it that we want to accomplish with our research paper, and what are we actually doing? As in 'real life,' do not make things too complicated.

CHAPTER 3
FORMING A PROJECT GROUP

The research paper may be written individually or in a group. If you write alone it is important that you frequently discuss your research project with other people.

If writing in a group, the first task is to decide with whom you want to write your research paper. Identifying the right people is essential because you are going to spend a substantial amount of time with them, and because the success of your research paper is heavily dependent on your project group.

Group work can be frustrating. Nevertheless, you have to remember that working in a group is an important part of your studies, not least for the simple reason that you are likely to be working in groups for the rest of your working career.

You can choose your group members based on either professional or *personal* criteria. Professional criteria may include choosing group members based on a common interest or topic focus. *Personal* criteria take personalities and working styles into consideration. Sometimes it is a good idea to consider both personal and professional criteria when choosing group members. Note that your best drinking friends are not always your best working colleagues.

ALIGN YOUR EXPECTATIONS

Whether you pick your own group members or your teacher places you in a group, it is very important to align the group members' expectations at the very beginning of the process. This is true both on the professional and personal levels. If you do not select your own group members, then it is even more important that you align the group's expectations and agree on a set of ground rules. When clarifying expectations, it is important to be honest about your knowledge (your background), your strengths and weaknesses, how you *can* and *will* contribute to the project, and your expectations of yourself and of your fellow group members. When clarifying expectations, you should discuss:

- What grade is the group striving for?
- How much time is each person able and willing to allocate to the group's work?
- Are social activities a part of the group's activities?
- How can and will each group member contribute to the project, taking into account each person's strengths and weaknesses?

MAKE RULES

The more people you are in your group, the more important it is to agree on a set of rules. Potential rules could include:

- What happens if a group member is consistently late to group meetings? How late is it acceptable to be?
- How should group meetings be run? Should a group member be appointed the leader at each meeting? Should a secretary be appointed at each meeting? Should minutes be taken?
- What quality of written work is expected before it can be presented to the group?
- What happens if deadlines are not kept?
- What is the procedure for expelling a group member?
- How should group members give feedback to each other? This goes both for the oral discussions and the written work. A good approach is to agree that when giving feedback to another group member (in a group discussion or when the group member has written something); the person offering the feedback should always try to come up with an alternative suggestion.
- How are decisions to be made? Should there be unanimity, majority, or consensus-based decision making that tries to avoid 'winners' and 'losers'?

In order to avoid problems in the group, try to be attentive to:

- dominance (i.e., people who talk too much and/or bully others);
- unequal workloads;
- cultural differences and language competencies;
- and assure that all group members are given time to provide their input at the group meetings (e.g., by taking turns).

FINAL ADVICE

- Sometimes it can be useful to schedule group meetings with strict time limits; for example, meetings with a maximum of one or two hours, just like meetings in private and public organizations.
- Discuss social problems and professional disagreements as soon as they appear. It is better to have a discussion at the beginning when the problem can still be solved, than later in the process when the conflict has escalated. Make a rule that it is acceptable for members to state if they are not satisfied with the quality of the written work or the way a group member is contributing to the discussions.
- In turns, choose one person in the group to pose the critical questions. This is especially relevant if the group consists of similar personality types.

CHAPTER 4
YOUR SUPERVISOR

Supervisors are very individual when it comes to how they supervise and what they look for in a research paper. It is important to recognize that supervisors stress different aspects and have different competencies. What they emphasize often depends on their own academic research field. External supervisors often emphasize the specific aspects with which *they* themselves are working.

In terms of how they supervise, some supervisors are *process* oriented and some supervisors are *product* oriented. Some supervisors almost see themselves as members of the students' work group and provide extensive input. Other supervisors act more like consultants, only providing answers to the questions actually posed by the students. They see the individual or group process as one of trial and error, where the students must learn from their mistakes.

In terms of qualifications, supervisors can be divided into two main groups: Those who are *experts* in their field and those who are *generalists*. The advantage of a supervisor who is an expert in the field you are studying is that she can provide you with qualified feedback on the topic of your RQ. The challenge is that your research paper could end up sounding like a conversation between those who are already familiar with the topic. The advantage of having a generalist is that she is an expert when it comes to the process of writing a research paper. The challenge is that you cannot expect her to give you extensive feedback on your field of study. Of course there are supervisors who are both experts and generalists.

The role of the supervisor is to:

- Make you think and question what you are doing.
- Give you academic guidance about theories, methods, and relevant literature.
- Get you back on the right track if you are going too far in the wrong direction.

The role of the supervisor is NOT to:

- Solve all of your problems for you.
- Act as an (older) group member who shares your project process.
- Proofread what you have written.
- Check if you have reproduced the theories correctly.

CHOOSING YOUR SUPERVISOR

If you can choose your own supervisor, it is a good idea to investigate your options first. Check what former students say and whether the supervisor seems to be particularly busy.

MAKE IT EASY FOR YOUR SUPERVISOR

If you want to get the most out of your supervisor, you have to communicate the focus of your research paper and your key challenges very precisely. This is much more difficult than most students imagine, largely because they are so engrossed in the complexities of their own project. Be sure to think through what you want to discuss with your supervisor and how you are going to present your questions before the meeting. In this respect, when working in a group, it is important to remember that your supervisor has not participated in any of the group discussions. This means that your supervisor only hears a fragment of these discussions.

As a general rule: make life as easy as possible for your supervisor. Most supervisors are very busy. They have a full-time job and some oversee more than twenty-five projects at a time.

In general you can expect that 'what comes in comes out.' In other words, the higher the quality of the material you send to your supervisor, the higher the quality of the feedback you will get from her. If the layout is miserable, chapter introductions and summaries are lacking, the spelling is bad, and the sentences make no sense it is difficult for the supervisor to give substantive feedback.

PRIOR TO EACH MEETING WITH YOUR SUPERVISOR

When you send documents to your supervisor prior to each meeting, you should:

- Specify what the supervisor has read before.
- Specify the key problems you want the supervisor to focus on.
- Specify the objectives of the meeting (i.e., what are the main problems you want the supervisor to consider and give her opinion on).
- Make sure that the language is understandable and readable.
- Make sure that long documents have a table of content and page numbers. Also, make sure that the chapters are connected and there are introductions for each chapter.

MEETING YOUR SUPERVISOR

It is always a good idea to meet with your supervisor early in the process, especially if you are in the first years of your studies when you do not have much experience writing research papers. Your supervisor can guide you in the right direction, so that you do not waste your time investigating a RQ that turns out not to constitute a real problem or working on a RQ for which it is almost impossible to find the appropriate data or theories.

When you meet with your supervisor for the first time, you have to align your expectations. This includes considering the following topics:

- The role of your supervisor.
- Your supervisor's expectations.
- The number of meetings your supervisor expects to have with you or your group.
- Which grade you are striving for.
- Your supervisor's strengths and weaknesses in relation to supervising your project.
- How many days in advance of each meeting you should send material to your supervisor.

- How to communicate with your supervisor between meetings (by phone, e-mail, etc.).
- The quality of the documents that you will send to your supervisor.

At the end of each meeting, agree on action points for the next meeting, a date when you will send new documents to your supervisor, and a date by which you will follow up on the things you talked about at the meeting. If your supervisor agrees to it, you may record the supervisory sessions, so that you can always double-check what the supervisor said.

WHAT STUDENTS EXPECT FROM THEIR SUPERVISOR

In order to align your expectations with your supervisor it may be useful to know what to expect (and demand) from a good supervisor. Based on numerous interviews with students, I have found that students appreciate when their supervisor:

- Is honest. What students seemingly hate the most are supervisors who say that everything is fine and then 'slaughter' their students at the examination.
- States what she believes to be a good research paper and what she looks for in a research paper. It is your supervisor who grades you at the exam, so it is important to know what she emphasizes.
- Responds quickly.
- Sets limits in terms of what she will read and what she will not read.
- Establishes clear expectations (this cuts both ways).
- Gets the student or group back on the right track if it is going towards a dead end.
- Provokes thoughtfulness.
- Is honest about her strengths and weaknesses.

PART 2
DURING

Having considered the project group and supervisor relations, we will now turn to the actual project work. This starts by defining the RQ and takes you through the various parts of the research paper.

CHAPTER 5
CHOOSING A RESEARH QUESTION (RQ)

Everything in a research paper must relate to the RQ. The RQ is by far the most important component of a research paper. It is the red thread that runs through the research paper, dictating what should be included and what should be excluded.

If you have a precise, logical, and well-formulated RQ, you will know exactly what to look for when researching and writing. The RQ becomes the glasses through which you sort information and organize your writing. The sharper the RQ, the better the glasses.

DIFFERENT TYPES OF RQS

There are many types of RQs. Here is a list of five different *conceptual* types of RQs (Andersen 2002: 22 ff):

- *Descriptive:* Describes a topic without trying to understand it. For example, how many Danes have an income of more than U.S. $ 50,000?
- *Problem identifying/explorative:* Investigates phenomena that you do not have much knowledge about with the purpose of identifying problems for further research. For example, what are the potential reasons that the organization has such a high employee turnover rate?
- *Explanatory/understanding:* Asks why certain phenomena take place. For example, is it because of the economic recession that we are currently seeing an increase in right-wing parties in Europe?
- *Problem solving/normative:* Goes one step further by developing potential solutions for the problem. For example, should the company B&O focus on research and development, LEAN, or branding to increase its profits?
- *Interventionist:* Returns to the original problem that the research paper investigated and suggests a solution. For example, how can the imple-

mentation of the new human resource strategy help decrease the employee turnover in the organization?

Within these conceptual types there are many different ways to approach a topic and thus formulate a RQ. Some RQs are purely *theoretical*; some deal with a *specific problem*, whereas others focus on *comparative studies*. Some RQs originate in a *paradox* or peculiarity, such as investigating why female cyclists are twice as likely to be killed in traffic as male cyclists.

Regardless of these differences, almost all RQs deal with some kind of *problem* that has to be solved, answered, or understood. Some research papers 'just' analyze the problem, while others also try to come up with solutions for the problems they identify.

HOW TO FIND A RELEVANT RQ

You can do a number of things to find inspiration for your RQ:

- Look for relevant and interesting topics in the media, such as in newspapers or international magazines like The Economist or Newsweek. You can look for topics that have been in the press recently or for newly released academic reports.
- Look at the texts and theories that you have been exposed to during your studies. You can identify potential problems in one or more of these texts and/or theories and use these as a starting point for your RQ.
- Search for research papers from previous years at your school's library. It may be helpful to browse research papers from a wide range of degree programs, including bachelors' projects and masters' theses.

When beginning the search for a potential RQ, start with light materials such as short articles, summaries of books, newspapers, or perhaps your textbook. At first, do not read thick books. It takes too much time. You can use the references in your initial sources to find additional relevant information. Seek out people who know something about the RQ you would like to write about. They could be professors, staff at government agencies, or other professionals.

Look for things that puzzle you. Look for dilemmas, paradoxes, uncertainties, and problems in general. For instance, Japan offers an interesting *puzzle and paradox*. The country was hit quite severely during the Asian crisis in the late 1990s and suffered a prolonged period of economic turbulence, yet life expectancy subsequently increased faster than at any time in the preceding two decades. Another paradox is why a country like Denmark is so bad at breaking the 'social inheritance'—i.e. why, despite the extensive Danish welfare system and free education, many young Danes from the lower social classes, do not take an education.

Look for problems with a high degree of *uncertainty* about potential solutions. The record industry's future could be a relevant topic to analyze, because no one knows how the record industry will evolve. This is partly because there are many different actors and partly because there are many unknown factors—especially technological factors. An example of a RQ related to the record industry could be: '*We will examine how the record company, EMI Group, as part of the record industry, is influenced and challenged by the increasing digitalization of society. Against this background, we will discuss and come up with concrete suggestions as to how EMI can create a business model that is profitable and competitive in a digital future.*'

Look for *economic and social problems*. If you identify a social problem, most of the time it is also an economic problem. A RQ about a social and economic problem could be: '*How do integration, social exclusion, and economic inequality in the form of unemployment affect the crime rate among ethnic minorities, and why are ethnic minorities responsible for a larger percentage of the criminal activity than natives in Denmark and the United Kingdom?*'

BRAINSTORM

Once you have done some preliminary research, have a brainstorming session with your group and create a list of all the different problems and potential RQs on which you could base your research paper. If you are writing on your own, try to find a colleague/fellow student with whom to brainstorm. When brainstorming:

- focus on quantity, not quality;
- withhold criticism and build on the ideas put forward by others;
- welcome unusual ideas;
- combine and improve ideas;
- and remember that every person and every idea has equal worth.

THREE CRITERIA FOR CHOOSING YOUR RQ

Next, choose which RQ you want to write about. I recommend my students to choose a RQ according to three criteria:

- Choose a RQ that is relevant and constitute a real problem. The best RQs are based on problems that are actually discussed in real life, for example, a problem a specific organization is actually facing. Using a real (and contemporary) problem makes the project more interesting to read.
- Choose a RQ that you find interesting. You have to work many hours with the RQ.
- Choose a RQ about which you expect to be able to obtain information.

CHOOSING YOUR ANALYTICAL PERSPECTIVE

RQs can be analyzed from many different disciplinary perspectives. A RQ about corporate social responsibility (CSR) could, for instance, be analyzed from the following perspectives:

- *Sociology:* Do the many new CSR-based partnerships constitute a new sociological trend/paradigm?
- *Law:* What is the legal status of CSR (i.e., soft law) compared to hard law?

- *Branding:* In which ways can the target organization brand itself using CSR?
- *Communication:* In which ways can the target organization communicate about CSR to its many stakeholders?
- *Economics:* In which ways can CSR create value for the target organization?
- *Human resources:* In which ways can the target organization use their CSR activities as a human resource tool?
- *Political science:* Is CSR the new version of corporatism?

It should be noted that you can analyze a RQ from more than one perspective.

CHOOSING THE SPECIFIC TOPIC (OF ANALYSIS)

Within each of these analytical perspectives, there are numerous specific topics you could choose. You can analyze each of the topics below from most of the abovementioned perspectives. For instance, all of the topics below can be analyzed from an economic or legal perspective. Using CSR again as a case example, you could write about the role of:

- CSR and partnerships (How do NGOs and companies most successfully enter into partnerships?).
- CSR and supply chains (How does an organization most optimally implement CSR throughout the supply chain?).
- CSR as an indication of a new rationality (Does CSR really constitute a new paradigm?).
- CSR and morality (Does CSR have anything to do with morality?).
- CSR and risk management (How can the organization use CSR as risk management?).
- CSR and lobbying (Can lobbying be considered good CSR?).
- CSR and stakeholders (How does an organization communicate CSR to its stakeholders?).

- CSR and corporate governance (What is the link between CSR and corporate governance?).
- CSR and profits (Does CSR really pay off?).

Again, you can choose to analyze more than one topic. However, if you analyze more than one topic, it is a good idea to specify which one is the most significant and why.

FORMULATING YOUR RQ

The Danish poet, writer, mathematician, and inventor Piet Hein said that the creative process is characterized by the fact that we cannot formulate a problem before we know its answer. Formulating a RQ is indeed a creative process; therefore, you should expect that your RQ can, and often will, change throughout the writing process as you or your group obtain more information about your chosen RQ.

You will most likely find that you are constantly refining and qualifying your RQ. Indeed, the RQ sometimes must be changed even at the very end of the writing process, to ensure that there is a direct link from the RQ to the conclusion. Some find themselves changing their RQ at the very end of the writing process because they realize that their RQ is not a real problem or that their analyses are in fact addressing a different question than the RQ poses.

There are several things to take into account when formulating a RQ:

- The RQ must be manageable within the given time horizon. That means you have to consider if you have the resources to analyze the RQ before the deadline. One of the biggest challenges is to formulate a RQ that is clear-cut. A very common problem is that students want to analyze too many aspects in their research paper.
- The RQ should be as concrete as possible. An overly broad RQ leads to a superficial treatment of the subject.
- Consider formulating a RQ you can measure. If the RQ is measurable then it will be easier to work with and draw conclusions.

- Ask if there are existing theories and empirical data you can use to analyze the RQ, and whether you have access to these.
- Also, consider if there are enough theories or other analytic tools that you can use to examine the RQ.
- Remember that every word in the RQ is important.

Make an effort to formulate your RQ into one sentence. Remember that you can supplement your RQ with sub-questions or hypotheses. However, if your RQ is comprised of two (or three) equally important problems (analytical focus areas) then it is okay to use more than one sentence to formulate your RQ.

When formulating a RQ remember to discuss the following:

- *What kind of problem is it?* There are many different types of problems: economic, political, sociological, environmental, theoretical, personal, et cetera.
- *Why is it a problem?* Is it a problem because there is ample media attention, because there is no media attention, because it might have some severe future economic consequences, or something else?
- *Who experiences the problem?* Is it a societal problem; a problem for a specific company or an NGO; a problem for a specific industry; a problem for a specific group or person, or someone else?
- *Who is your audience?* In other words, to whom is the research paper relevant? The type of problem you are analyzing is linked to its intended audience. Is the research paper relevant for national politicians, your professor, a CEO or her employees, a particular industry, your fellow students, or someone else?

When formulating a RQ try to avoid:

- *Yes/No questions.* For example, 'Is unemployment rising in the United Kingdom compared to the US?' Or, 'Are working-class students less likely to go to university than middle-class students?' Yes/no questions usually lead to discussions and analyses where the nuances disappear.

- *Descriptive questions.* For example, 'What are the differences between the education systems in Spain and France?' The pro and con discussions are usually left out if you choose a descriptive RQ.

The nature of the RQ depends on how much knowledge you have about your chosen topic. A RQ such as *'Why is there such a significant difference in intergenerational social mobility between Denmark and England?'* indicates that you have some knowledge about the topic because it suggests that you already know that there are differences in intergenerational social mobility between Denmark and England. The more knowledge you have about the topic, the narrower your research question can be.

WHEN YOU HAVE SETTLED ON A RQ

When you have settled on your RQ you should present a preliminary table of contents for the entire research paper to your supervisor. Use typical chapter headlines such as methodology, theories, analysis, and conclusion, and briefly describe what you expect the various chapters to contain. This provides you and your supervisor with a rough picture of the final research paper. If you and/or your supervisor have a clear picture of the entire research paper, it is often an indication that the final research paper is going to be good. Making a table of contents for your project can also give you an overview of the workload and thus help you to make a project plan and distribute the work among group members.

FINAL ADVICE

- Before settling on your RQ, double-check that it fulfills the formal requirements and learning objectives in your study handbook. If you are in doubt, ask your supervisor.
- Spend substantial time formulating the RQ. One week used to identify a good and relevant RQ can save much more time during the subsequent writing process. If the RQ is unclear the resulting research paper is almost certainly going to be unclear.

- Show your RQ to somebody outside the group and ask if they think it is precise and understandable.
- Do not decide what your conclusions will be at the outset. Be critical of yourself and your findings throughout the process. Many students decide on a RQ where they know, or think they know, the answer in advance. This negatively affects the entire research process, mainly because the arguments and discussions tend to become artificial.

CHAPTER 6
FORMING ASSUMPTIONS, SUB-QUESTIONS, AND HYPOTHESES

In the course of proposing and investigating a RQ, some students use sub-questions, others hypotheses, and still others rely on assumptions. You can choose whether or not you want to work with hypotheses and/or sub-questions; however, most research papers benefit from working with hypotheses and/or sub-questions, because they structure the research process and hence the research paper.

It is important to note that there are considerable differences between assumptions, sub-questions, and hypotheses.

ASSUMPTIONS

An assumption is an underlying premise upon which the entire research paper is based. An example of an assumption is when a group bases their RQ and the subsequent analysis in the context of the 'risk society' or the 'negotiating society'. Another example of an assumption is that people are rational and utility maximizing, as neoclassical economic theory asserts. The assumption could also be that people are *not* rational and utility maximizing, as more and more academics assert. You do not necessarily have to investigate or prove whether your assumptions are correct, but you should account for why you have chosen them.

SUB-QUESTIONS

A sub-question is when you break your RQ into smaller analytical problems. It can be advantageous to use sub-questions if your RQ is broad and consists of several minor empirical and/or theoretical problems. Analyzing and answering the sub-questions helps answering your overall RQ.

As an example take a look at the following RQ: '*In which ways can Voss*

Water improve its CSR strategy during a time with increasing global focus on the earth's limited water resources?' In order to answer this RQ you could analyze the following sub-questions:

- What is the current CSR strategy of Voss Water?
- Do the CSR activities of the Voss Foundation create a positive image of Voss Water?
- In which ways is the CSR strategy of Voss Water reflected in their financial performance?
- Compared to other bottled water firms, how is Voss Water positioned with respect to the social issue of high water scarcity?

HYPOTHESES

A hypothesis is a preliminary answer (some define it as a working question) to your RQ that is based on your present knowledge. A good or qualified hypothesis is based on theories and/or empirical observations, and not just on your own assumptions. Remember when choosing which hypotheses to work with that you have to be able to prove or disprove these hypotheses, or at least it has to be *plausible* that the hypothesis can be proved or disproved. Proving or disproving the hypotheses takes place in your analysis, but also remember that your hypotheses have to be addressed in your conclusion.

One advantage of working with hypotheses is that they help narrow down the areas of analysis. If you work with hypotheses, I recommend that you formulate a maximum of four; otherwise, you run the risk of a superficial analysis. For that reason some supervisors also recommend that you only work with one or two hypotheses at most.

Once you have settled on your RQ, brainstorm and list all the potential hypotheses that are relevant to your RQ. Below is an example of *some* of the potential hypotheses relevant to the RQ, 'Why did the world's biggest retail company, Wal-Mart, enter China successfully, but failed in Germany?':

- Wal-Mart succeeded in China because they had a thorough knowledge of *Chinese shopping culture*.
- Wal-Mart succeeded in China because the *competition* was very limited.
- Wal-Mart succeeded in China because they adapted their *business model* according to the *Chinese culture* in general.
- Wal-Mart failed in Germany because they did not enter into *cooperative agreements* or *partnerships*.
- Wal-Mart failed in Germany because the company applied the wrong branding strategy.
- *Wal-M*art failed in Germany because the *logistical and geographical structure* was different from that of the United States.
- Wal-Mart failed in Germany because the *competition* was too fierce.

CHOOSE THE HYPOTHESES WITH THE GREATEST EXPLANATORY POWER

After listing all of the potential hypotheses, discuss which of these you want to analyze. The hypotheses you choose to analyze should be those you believe—with the knowledge you have from the beginning of the research process—have the greatest explanatory power in relation to your RQ. In the Wal-Mart example above, this would mean choosing those hypotheses you believe were the *main reasons* for the relative success and failure of Wal-Mart.

I recommend my students to list the most important hypotheses they decided *not to analyze* in the methodology chapter. Since you did not investigate all the potential hypotheses, the conclusion you end up with is only part of the answer.

FINAL ADVICE

- Define the key words in the hypotheses and sub-questions you use.
- Always answer the hypotheses and sub-questions. This should take

place in both the conclusion and in those chapters where you analyze each hypothesis or sub-question.
- ▸ You can change the hypotheses and sub-questions during the writing process as you learn more about your RQ. You can also decide not to include one or more of the hypotheses and/or sub-questions in the final research paper.

CHAPTER 7
PLANNING THE RESEARCH PROCESS

Planning the research process from the beginning positively affects the final result.

Once you have settled on your RQ and hypotheses/sub-questions, be sure to plan the rest of your research process before you start writing. Writing long research papers requires careful planning; many students are surprised to find that three months is not much time. Most students and groups work almost non-stop the last forty-eight hours leading up to the deadline. This often negatively affects the final result. Remember that it is equally important that you plan your research process even when writing short research papers, where you only have two or three weeks.

Plan according to major deadlines and adjust the plan if necessary. Make a 'backward plan'. A 'backward plan' is when you first set the date you wish to hand in the research paper, then which days you plan to do the final editing, then which days you plan to write your conclusion etc. It is important that you finish writing *at least* a couple of days before handing in the research paper because you need time for editing, to summarize its conclusions, check for spelling, references, and so forth. The final fine-tuning process is very time-consuming. Plan so you have a minimum of two whole days for editing a sixty-five to eighty page research paper. If possible, plan it so you are done writing a week or two before the deadline. This way you have extra time if something does not go according to plan. If working in a group, make sure to divide the work between the members of the group. It is a good idea to assign each member his or her own specific tasks. It is important that you are *very clear and specific* when you delegate individual assignments.

A TYPICAL RESEARCH PAPER

A long research paper of sixty five to eighty pages should, *on average*, have the following number of pages allocated to each of the chapters:

- Executive summary: one to two pages
- Introduction: two to three pages
- RQ: two to three pages
- Methodology: seven to eight pages
- Empirical data (including a description of the object of analysis): ten to twelve pages
- Theory: fifteen pages
- Analysis: twenty pages
- Conclusion: two to five pages
- Future perspectives: two to three pages
- Table of contents, list of literature, appendices, etc.: ten pages

If you are sufficiently self-confident, you can contemplate structuring your research paper in a different way. Most examiners have read so many 'standard projects' that they would probably find it interesting to read a research paper with a new approach. The more experienced and self-confident you become in writing research papers, the better this idea becomes. Still, only do it if it makes sense.

FINAL ADVICE

- For many students, forty to eight pages seems to be an almost impossible amount to write. To overcome this, a good advice is to collect as much information as you can in the beginning and then start writing without thinking too much about the sentences and formulations.
- If you have sufficient time at the end of the research process, set the research paper aside for two to three days and then edit it with fresh and critical eyes.
- One way to organize the writing process is to agree that when one group member has written something, another group member will read, comment, and/or rewrite it using the 'track changes' function.

CHAPTER 8
THE INTRODUCTION

The introduction is the first chapter the examiner reads in more detail; hence, it is important that the introduction is sharp, precise, and to the point so the examiner gets a good first impression of the research paper.

A good introduction establishes the context of the entire research paper and convinces the examiner that the RQ is relevant and interesting. Most students write the introduction at the end of the writing process. My advice, however, is the contrary: once you have decided on a RQ, it is a good idea to write the introduction. Doing this will help you see your research problem more clearly and, as a consequence, aid you in focusing your research paper.

To arouse interest, consider beginning with an anecdote, stating an interesting new angle on the problem, or presenting some eye-catching statistics or controversial points from the media.

CHAPTER 9
METHODOLOGY

The methodology chapter is one of the most important chapters. It explains *how* you are analyzing your RQ, *how* the research paper is structured, and even more importantly it explains *why* the research paper is structured as it is and the consequences of the numerous methodological choices that were made during the writing process.

Despite the importance of methodological choices and the methodological approach, many students do not use much space or energy explaining the methodological aspects of their research paper. This is most likely because they are a bit uncertain about the purpose and relative importance of methodology. This uncertainty is perhaps also the reason why most students use their methodology section to describe *what* they have done rather than *why* they have done it. The difference is enormous.

WHAT IS METHODOLOGY?

I define methodology as the choices the student or group makes about how to seek information, the techniques used to collect it, how to conduct the analysis, how to structure the information in the research paper, and the consequences of all these choices on the overall conclusions of the research paper. Thus, methodology includes the methods, procedures, and techniques used to collect, analyze, and structure information. In more philosophical terms, I define methodology as the art of structuring information chaos.

WHY METHODOLOGY?

Your methodological choices have a huge impact on the final conclusions of your research paper. When you choose to analyze one hypothesis, you exclude another. When you include some information, you exclude other information. When you choose one theory, you exclude another. When you choose to analyze one organization and exclude another, you will obtain different results. When you interview one expert, you get his more or less biased view. If you had interviewed another expert you would probably have received another view on the topic/problem. Consequently, it is important to account for all the major choices you make during the project. This accounting is made in the methodology chapter.

Accounting for your methodological choices is important because it is common that two research papers analyzing the same RQ will end up with completely opposite conclusions, depending on their methodological approach and the sources on which they base their analysis.

Since a RQ can be answered in many different ways, you can structure your research paper almost any way you want, as long as you offer good methodological arguments to support your choices.

THE CONTENTS OF THE METHODOLOGY CHAPTER

In the methodology chapter, you should account for the following aspects, which will be explained below:

- Your philosophy of science (including epistemology and ontology).
- Your overall methodological approach (i.e., inductive or deductive).
- Your delimitations (i.e., your methodological choices).
- Your empirical data (qualitative and/or quantitative).
- Your choice of theories (including critique).
- The structure of the research paper.
- The validity and reliability of the research paper.
- The literature review.
- Definition of key terms.

THE PHILOSOPHY OF SCIENCE (INCLUDING EPISTEMOLOGY AND ONTOLOGY)

Here you explain which philosophy of science you have chosen, why you chose this philosophical approach, and the resulting methodological consequences. This discussion mainly relates to the origin of the theories you have chosen. Some of the most important philosophical approaches include: positivism, social constructivism, realism, interpretivism (hermeneutics), and pragmatism (critical theory) (Bryman 2004).

In accounting for the philosophy of science, you could also account for the *ontology* and *epistemology*. *Ontology* deals with questions concerning which entities exist or can be said to exist, and how such entities can be grouped. Principal questions of ontology include: 'What can be said to exist?' and 'Into what categories, if any, can we sort existing things?' *Epistemology*, or theory of knowledge, is the branch of philosophy concerned with the nature and scope of knowledge. It addresses questions like: 'What is knowledge?', 'How is knowledge acquired?', 'What can we be sure of?', 'How do we get beyond mere opinion to real knowledge?', and 'How do we know what we know?' (Bryman 2004).

THE OVERALL METHODOLOGICAL APPROACH (I.E., INDUCTIVE OR DEDUCTIVE)

You should account for the way you approach your RQ. There are two fundamentally different ways you can approach a RQ:

- An inductive approach, which is also called a knowledge-based or 'bottom-up' approach.
- A deductive approach, which is also called a rule-based or 'top-down' approach.

An *inductive approach* is where you try to develop a theory out of your empirical data. Here you build a theory. Inductive reasoning moves from specific observations to broader generalizations to theories. You start with making empirical observations. Based on these observations you look for patterns that often lead to tentative hypotheses. Upon these tentative hypotheses, you build your theory. This process can be described as climbing a hill. An example of an inductive approach is when you want to construct your own theory about the potentially important role of culture in creating economic growth based on, for instance, interviews and/or empirical surveys.

A *deductive approach* works from a general level to a more specific level. Here you test a theory. You start from the top by selecting one or more theories to apply to your RQ. Based on these theories you collect empirical data in order to analyze to what extent these empirical findings support or contradict your theories. An example of a deductive approach is when you want to test a theory that claims culture plays an important role in creating economic growth.

The difference between the inductive and deductive approaches is that a deductive approach requires you to discuss your empirical findings in the context of the theories you are using. With an inductive approach, you discuss your tentative theory in comparison to your empirical findings and also in comparison to what other theorists have written about the topic and your theory.

THE DELIMITATIONS (I.E., YOUR METHODOLOGICAL CHOICES)

It is very important to account for the delimitations you have chosen and their methodological consequences. Delimitations are essentially about what you could have done differently in answering your RQ, but decided not to do.

It is important that the delimitations are related to your RQ and not just contextual delimitations. Examples of contextual delimitations include: '*We only have seventy pages at our disposal so we cannot go in-depth with our RQ,*' or '*We only have three months so we do not have as much time as we would have liked.*' The amount of pages and the time you have to write your research paper are always set. Methodology is consequently about making the best choices based on the data, theories, time, and resources you have.

Research problems (i.e., RQs) are normally caused by numerous different factors. Most—if not all—research papers analyze only a few of the factors that could have caused, or could explain, the problem they are investigating.

You must account for the factors you chose to analyze and why you chose these factors. You should also account for the factors you did not analyze and why you did not analyze them. Finally, you should consider whether you would have reached a different conclusion by analyzing an alternate set of factors. In short, you must account for the delimitations you have made and the methodological consequences of those delimitations. Some examples of delimitations include:

- *Time period:* 'We only analyzed the organization during a specific period of time.' (The time period could have been chosen because an important event took place with respect to the organization).
- *Geography:* 'We only analyzed certain countries, regions, cities, industries, cultures, people or organizations.'
- *Hypotheses:* 'We only analyzed three out of the eight hypotheses we came up with in our brainstorming session.'
- *Theories:* 'We only used two theories.' (The theories may have been chosen because there was significant debate about them, because they are the most well known, or because they are the most relevant to answering your RQ).
- *Cases:* 'We only analyzed two cases, rather than five.'
- *Analytical context:* 'We analyzed our RQ in the context of the risk society and not in the context of a negotiation society.'
- *Empirical sources:* 'We only used certain newspapers as the basis for our analysis' and/or 'We only interviewed people living in Copenhagen.'

THE EMPIRICAL DATA (QUALITATIVE AND/OR QUANTITATIVE DATA)

You should also account for which types of empirical data you are using, why you are using them, and their validity. There are two overarching types of empirical data: qualitative and quantitative. *Qualitative data* is often called 'soft data,' while *quantitative data* is referred to as 'hard data.' *Qualitative* data could be minutes from meetings, individual texts, laws and rules, pictures, videos, and observation notes. *Quantitative* data could be surveys and statistics, opinion pools, and so forth.

It is important to be critical about the quality of the data you are collecting. Even though the Western countries has some of the best and most valid statistics in the world, these quantitative statistics can still be criticized on a number of grounds. To ensure objectivity, validity and reliability in your quantitative and qualitative data see Bryman 2004.

CHOICE OF THEORIES (INCLUDING CRITIQUE)

In the methodological chapter it is common to discuss your choice of theories, including their strengths and weaknesses in relation to answering your RQ, and perhaps why you chose these particular theories as opposed to others. You should also critique the theories you are using. This critique may be located in the chapter on theory or in the analysis. The description of your theoretical approach should be elaborated by a summary of the theories. This should take place in the chapter on theory or in the analysis (see below).

STRUCTURE OF THE RESEARCH PAPER

It is a good idea to account for the overall structure of your research paper. Many students give both a written and a graphical outline (a figure) of the project structure so the examiner has both a descriptive and a visual idea of the research paper's structure.

VALIDITY AND RELIABILITY

It is important to account for *validity* and *reliability*, both because an objective truth does not exist in the social sciences and because your methodological choices have a considerable impact on the validity and reliability of your research paper.

Validity: There are two types of validity: internal and external. *Internal validity* refers to the *credibility* of the research paper. The reason for accounting for internal validity is to see whether you tested or measured what you intended to test or measure. Internal validity occurs when it can be concluded that there is a causal relationship between the variables being studied. A danger is that changes might be caused by other factors; thus, you have to use valid research methods, and you have to be able to carefully explain the study's background, objective, and the research method used.

External validity refers to the degree to which the conclusions can be *generalized* across social settings. Put more simply, external validity is the degree to which the conclusions in your study would hold for other persons in other places and at other times. For students working with qualitative data, external validity represents a problem, because they have a tendency to employ case studies and/or small samples that often cannot be generalized. To heighten validity, use the newest sources, the original sources, and the main academic sources.

Reliability: Reliability refers to the degree to which a research study can be replicated. The conclusions of your research paper should be reliable such that other researchers would find the same results if they used the same methodological approaches. Consequently, reliability is difficult to obtain in qualitative research because it is impossible to 'freeze' the social setting and the specific circumstances.

Your qualitative and quantitative data will almost always have flaws and/or be biased. However, it does not matter too much if your data has flaws as long as you are aware of this fact and account for its consequences with respect to validity and reliability. An example: You only succeeded in getting one interview, and furthermore the interview is with a (probably) biased person from the organization you are analyzing. Consequently, you have to estimate the extent to which you can trust what the person said and judge how much only one interview is worth in terms of the overall external validity of the research paper. In short: you have to account for what the empirical data is and what the empirical data is not.

THE LITERATURE REVIEW

A literature review identifies the main academic texts and authors related to your field of investigation (i.e., your RQ); it provides an overview of your chosen research field. When you conduct a literature review, you generate state-of-the-art knowledge about your specific RQ. The literature review gives an overview of the main things that have been written about your RQ. It is often included in the methodology chapter, but it can also be placed earlier in the research paper. Some students do not include a literature review in their research paper at all.

Writing a good literature review is an extensive task, but you will be rewarded later in the process if you do it. The literature review can also be useful for qualifying your RQ and hypotheses.

DEFINITION OF KEY TERMS

A glossary of the key terms used in your research paper is often included in the chapter on methodology. For instance: Is *legitimacy* the same as *credibility*? And what is the difference between *marketing, communication,* and *branding*?

FINAL ADVICE

- ▶ Use a logbook so you can see all the methodological choices you have made throughout your research process.
- ▶ Do not write in retrospect. All chapters should be written as if they were the last chapter, including the methodology chapter. This means that when you write the methodology chapter you know all the choices you have made throughout the research process, and their consequences.
- ▶ Use the same terminology throughout the entire research paper, not least in the headings. Using different words to describe the same phenomena is very confusing for the examiner.
- ▶ Some universities require students to write an individual project report about their experiences and lessons learned. If so, do yourself a big fa-

vor and read some of the individual project reports that last year's students have written. This will help you to avoid some of the mistakes they made.

CHAPTER 10
USING EMPIRICAL DATA

Some research papers have a separate chapter in which all the empirical data is presented. However, if you place all the empirical data in a separate chapter, there is a risk of having to repeat much of the data again in the analysis. To avoid this, some students give only an overall description of their data in a separate chapter, and then include the relevant details in the analysis. Other students do not have a separate chapter at all and include only the relevant empirical data in their analysis. Do what you consider to be most logical for your research paper.

QUALITATIVE AND QUANTITATIVE DATA

As described above there are two overarching types of empirical data: qualitative and quantitative. *Qualitative data* is descriptive and is often called 'soft data', while quantitative data is numeric and is referred to as 'hard data'.

Examples of *qualitative* data include answers from individual interviews, minutes from meetings, individual texts, laws and rules, pictures, videos, and observation notes.

Examples of *quantitative* data include the GDP of a nation state, surveys and statistics, opinion pools, the number of intoxicated Swedes in a bar in Copenhagen on a given Friday night, or the height and weight of a particular person.

Whether you use qualitative or quantitative data depends on your specific RQ. However, there are some important contrasts between quantitative and qualitative research. Some of the chief distinguishing features between the two approaches are: Quantitative research is typically highly structured, whereas qualitative research is invariably unstructured. Quantitative research is typically used on a macro level, whereas qualitative research operates on a micro level. Quantitative research is typically concerned with generalizations, whereas qualitative research is concerned with a contextual understanding.

When answering your RQ, it is sometimes advantageous to use both quantitative and qualitative data because they can supplement each other. But again, this choice depends on your specific RQ.

FINAL ADVICE

- Data collecting is always time consuming and making your own quantitative or qualitative questionnaire is very time consuming. If you contemplate making a questionnaire/survey, be sure that you have the time and resources to do so. If you want to make your own survey, a place to start is www.surveymonkey.com.
- It is a good idea to find additional academic literature and not just use literature contained in the course binder or from the Internet.
- Remember that you only have a limited number of pages. For example, if you are writing your research paper about a specific organization, do not use too much space describing its history (unless this is particularly relevant to your research paper).
- Always consider whether you can place less significant information in the appendices, taking into consideration that often appendices are not read.

CHAPTER 11
CHOOSING AND USING THEORIES

There are, fundamentally, two ways of presenting your theories. One way is to give an elaborate summary of your theories in the theoretical chapter. This is a very common approach; however, it includes a risk of creating repetition in the analysis section.

The other way is to include only a brief summary of the main points of your theories in the theoretical chapter and then include the remaining aspects in the analysis. The summary can then be on a more conceptual level, with the challenge being to reproduce only the context in which the theories are situated and *the main points* of the theory.

Write the summary of the theories in your own words. This increases your chances of understanding them too. It is often a good idea to include examples in the theoretical summary to illustrate the theoretical points.

Here it is worth repeating: Only include those parts of the theory that are relevant to answering your RQ.

WHAT IS A THEORY?

Working with theory is probably the main thing that differentiates this process from previous learning experiences. It is therefore of crucial importance that you know what a theory is and how to use it.

So what is a theory? The word 'theory' derives from the Greek *theorein*, which means 'to look at.' When constructing theories, academics look at—and collect empirical data about—how the world operates. A theory is normally constructed on the basis of multiple empirical surveys. You could say that theory simplifies our complex world in order to understand it. As a result, many theories are constructed so that organizations (companies, politicians, and decision makers in general) have guidelines on how to act in this complex globalized world.

One can roughly divide theories into *social science* theories and *natural science* theories. An example of a natural science theory is Isaac Newton's theory of universal gravitation. As you might guess, this book will concentrate on social science theories.

Theories exist on different levels. For example, theories exist on a personal level. I can have my own theory that my best friend is insecure despite his seemingly very confident behavior. I can have a theory that for economic development to take place in developing countries, a majority of their national leaders must be committed to national economic growth. These 'personal theories' are based on my own knowledge and my own experiences, rather than on extensive empirical surveys. For a more elaborate/theoretical outline about the different levels on which theories can be constructed, see Reynolds 2007.

Princeton University defines a more formal theory this way: A theory is a 'well-substantiated explanation of some aspect of the natural world; an organized system of accepted knowledge that applies in a variety of circumstances to explain a specific set of phenomena' (wordnetweb.princeton.edu/perl/webwn). More formal or professional theories are based on comprehensive surveys, or, in other words, the systematic collection of empirical data (qualitative interviews and/or quantitative questionnaires) that answer questions about how the world behaves.

Students often ask if the result of a single empirical survey is a theory. My answer is 'no', but it can be the beginning of a more formal theory. Many also ask if a model is a theory. My answer is a yes-and-no. For instance the PESTEL-model—a strategic tool for understanding e.g. market growth or decline—builds on numerous empirical surveys, and could be classified as a theory. However, there is a difference between a 'real theory' and a model. The difference is that a 'real theory' normally predicts something, in other words there is a causal element. Nevertheless, the difference is mostly insignificant, and you can use both theories and models in your research paper. It is also acceptable to use a single empirical survey and/or an article based on a single empirical survey as a substitute for theories *if* there are no theories related to your RQ.

CRITIQUING THEORIES

Some students include the critique of the theories in the theoretical chapter, while others include it in the analysis, or in the chapter on methodology. However, because theories are only simplified models of the world you have to be critical about the ones you are using. It is very important to be aware of their limitations.

As a rule of thumb, theories are generic, not specific: this makes them easy prey for critique. Below are some of the aspects you should take into account when critiquing theories:

- Consider when theories have been wrong or when two or more theories have come up with completely different conclusions.
- Consider whether the academic who created the theory focused only on her own research area and did not include other important areas that could be of equal relevance.
- Consider whether the theory is based on past circumstances and is thus outdated?
- Consider whether the theory is based on a population dissimilar to the one you are studying. Can a theory based on the experiences of Western countries be applied to developing ones? Can a theory based on Danish companies be used to explain something about American ones?
- Consider whether the basic assumptions that normative theories rely on are correct.
- Consider whether the theory is difficult to test.
- Consider whether the empirical data used to construct the theory is valid.
- Consider whether the theory is too simple or too abstract. Is it, for example, possible to construct a viable theory about an entity as complex as a nation-state?
- Consider the political convictions of the academic who created the theory and consider her specific methodological approaches. These are two aspects that profoundly influence the way the theory is constructed.

When critiquing a theory, start by finding other academics that have critiqued the theory. Wikipedia often has a list of prominent critics of the theory in question. Use the references from Wikipedia for further searching. Also, ask your supervisor if she can help you find critiques. All of this is important, but nothing matters more than using your common critical sense.

EXAMPLES OF THEORETICAL CRITIQUES

The critique can be on a conceptual and/or specific level. Again, do what seems most logical given your specific circumstances.

Your conceptual critique could focus on the ontology, epistemology, or basic assumptions underlying the theory. An example of a conceptual critique is a critique of the basic assumptions underlying neoclassical economic theory, namely that people are rational and utility maximizing. Another conceptual critique directed at neoclassical theory is that it has too much of a normative bias (Stiglitz 2001).

When criticizing a theory in more detail, you should come up with specific examples that contradict what the theory says. Another example of a more specific critique is the criticism of Michael Porter's Diamond model—a model that contributed to our understanding of the competitive position of a nation in global competition—for, among other things, using old empirical data, being constructed before the Internet came into existence, and not taking the importance of globalization sufficiently into account (Davies 2000).

HOW TO EMPLOY THEORIES

Theories can be used for many different purposes. You can:

- Use the theory to answer or explain your RQ
- Test the explanatory power of the theory in relation to your RQ
- Test the validity and/or truth of the theory based on your or others' empirical data, or by testing the theory using other theories

- Test two theories against each other to see which is more valid and/or has the most explanatory power

USE DIFFERENT THEORIES TO ANSWER THE SAME RQ

You can use different theories to solve your RQ. If you have a RQ that analyzes why there are such big differences in attitudes towards immigrants in Denmark, Sweden, and the United States, you can use different theories to answer that RQ. For instance, you can use discourse analysis theories, theories of town planning, theories of culture, historically based theories, and so forth. Or, you can use these different theories together. The choice of theory depends on the specific nature of your RQ.

CHAPTER 12
ANALYSIS

The analysis forms the main part of the research paper. This is where you get the chance to demonstrate that you can think critically, analytically, structurally, and independently.

In the analysis, you discuss and interpret the pros and cons related to answering your RQ. This has to be based on your theories, your empirical data, similar cases, what other academics and experts have said about your RQ, and your own analytic skills.

Always relate the discussion in the analysis section to your RQ, and always use your theories and empirical data in your analysis. A recurring problem in the analysis is that the theories and empirical data are not used to answer the RQ. Only include information relevant to the RQ. Research papers that contain too much irrelevant information display a fundamental lack of understanding of what a good research paper is. Just because something is interesting does not necessarily make it relevant.

In terms of structuring the analysis you can take your point of departure from your RQ, your hypotheses, your sub-questions, theories, or the characteristics of the object of analysis.

After reading your analysis, the examiner should have a good overview of the *key challenges* facing the object of analysis.

FINAL ADVICE

- The bulk of the analysis should be based on your theories and other scientifically based material. Even so, it is always good practice to state your own opinion in the analysis. This demonstrates that you are able to think independently. But when stating your own opinion, be sure to explicitly write that it is your own opinion. To support your opinions, describe similar cases where prominent academics have taken the same approach.

- It is a good idea to incorporate related cases as examples (e.g., from other countries or sectors) and examples in general. This adds quality to the analysis, demonstrates knowledge of things outside of the course literature, and shows an ability to think abstractly.
- If you conduct more than one analysis, try to use the conclusions from the various analyses actively in the subsequent analyses.

CHAPTER 13
THE CONCLUSION

In the conclusion, *always answer your RQ*. The first thing most examiners do is to read the RQ and the conclusion. For this reason alone it is a huge problem if you do not answer your RQ in the conclusion.

The conclusion summarizes the *main* findings of the research paper in relation to the RQ. The *length* of the conclusion can differ widely depending on what you include. Some integrate the analysis and discussion into the conclusion. Of course, this makes the conclusion rather long. In a research paper between forty and eighty pages a typical conclusion is two to four pages.

The 'truth' is very rarely black or white. This also goes for your conclusions; however, many students have a tendency to cast their conclusions in extreme terms. It is *acceptable to completely reject your RQ*, but ask yourself if this is in accordance with your analysis.

Likewise, if you work with hypotheses, it is completely *acceptable to reject your hypotheses*. However, it is very rare that a hypothesis can be confirmed with one hundred percent certainty. Instead, try to elaborate on which hypotheses have the strongest or weakest explanatory power with respect to your RQ. In doing so, you can use sentences such as 'there is a strong indication that hypothesis number three has the strongest/weakest explanatory power.' But again, it is acceptable to say that all—or some—of your hypotheses were wrong and did not have any explanatory power at all.

If you come up with solutions to a problem addressed in your RQ, do not simply conclude that e.g. an organization should 'just' implement this or that strategy to solve its problem(s). Remember to elaborate on *how* the organization should do this and address the potential problems associated with the suggested approach. If problems were so easily solved, the CEO or politicians would probably already have solved them. Remember the complexity of the world, and that the world is growing more complex by the day. Along the same lines, if you come up with solutions in relation to the RQ, I recommend that you prioritize these solutions, rather than simply listing them in random order.

FINAL ADVICE

- Make the conclusion easy to read. You can use bullets to list the most important findings. If you have more than one hypothesis, use small headings to make a conclusion for each of them.
- Repeat your RQ at the beginning of the conclusion—it will make the conclusion easier to read. Try to answer the RQ in one sentence. This forces you to identify and consider the essence of your work.

CHAPTER 14
FUTURE PERSPECTIVE

Some research papers include a chapter on future perspectives for the RQ. It is not obligatory, but sometimes it can add a nice final touch. The chapter about future perspectives usually elaborates on the RQ and tries to extrapolate from your conclusions.

Some future perspectives chapters elaborate on how a subsequent research paper concerning the same RQ could deal with the question. Another possibility is to adapt the conclusions from your study of a specific organization to another organization. You could also present your own solutions to the problem you have investigated. However, if you present your own solutions, try to find other cases or other theories to back them up and make sure that they are thought through and realistic. Revolutionary solutions are often unrealistic solutions. Put yourself in the position of the leader of the organization and ask yourself the question: 'Would I implement these solutions?'

You could also elaborate on your suggestions for future research. I.e., what needs to be done and/or analyzed in order to improve the theory you have used/analyzed in your research paper.

CHAPTER 15
EXECUTIVE SUMMARY

The executive summary should be placed at the very beginning of the research paper. I prefer to have it before the table of contents. Remember that the executive summary should give a concise picture of the overall research paper, the context of the research paper, and the main findings.

Try putting the research paper away before writing the executive summary. Remember that the examiner often does not have any idea what she is going to read about in your research paper, so the executive summary is a very important introduction to your work.

CHAPTER 16
LAYOUT AND LANGUAGE

Some examiners read thirty research papers or more, which cumulatively can easily exceed 2500 pages. So make it easy for the examiner to read your research paper. The examiner normally only reads your research paper one time, and sometimes that reading will be rather fast and cursory. Consequently, your research paper should be easy to read, and it should be easy to get an overall idea of the content.

THE LAYOUT

Everything you do that makes your research paper easy for the examiner to read is good. For example:

- Use headings and subheadings. Use headings that illustrate the chapter they introduce. The advantage of using headings is twofold: Not only do they make it easier for the examiner to get an overview, but they also discipline and structure your text. You can always delete some of the sub-headings in the final editing.
- Make sure that the table of contents is understandable and that it gives a good overview of the content. Looking at a well-structured table of contents gives the examiner a good first impression of what your project is about.
- Mention the RQ at the beginning of the research paper, not on page ten. Highlight the RQ so the examiner knows it is your RQ.
- Write a short introduction (two to three sentences) for each chapter so the examiner knows what she is going to read.
- Write a short sub-conclusion at the end of every important chapter.
- Use graphs, tables, and figures when possible.
- Use references when you have quoted something or when you refer to important findings. Rather one reference too many than one too few.

- Remember page numbers.
- Create a header in the margin or on top of each page so the examiner always knows which chapter she is reading.

THE LANGUAGE

- Use language that everybody understands. There is no need to make it more difficult than it is. Your friends and family should be able to understand your research paper without referencing a dictionary.
- Check the spelling. A project with spelling mistakes leaves a bad impression that will influence your grade negatively.
- Write short sentences. Long sentences are often difficult to read.
- If you are using difficult words or key terms, be sure that you know precisely what they mean and be sure that everybody in the group understands them in the same way.
- When describing difficult theories and concepts, try to describe these using your own words.
- Also, be sure to define the key words and key terms the first time you use them.
- There is no need to write in an academic style. Find your own writing style, and make sure that the style is coherent throughout the project. If working in a group let other group members rewrite what you have written and vice versa.
- Ask yourself if you enjoy reading what you have written; if not, then rewrite it.
- Avoid words like 'it' and 'they' when writing, but mention specifically what you are referring to.

QUOTATION, PLAGIARISM, AND REFERENCING

Plagiarism is the submission or presentation of work made by others as one's own. Whether intended or not, plagiarism is theft and, as such, is treated as a very serious violation of examination procedures. In order to avoid accusations of plagiarism, use references as often as possible.

There are several ways of referencing. I normally recommend the Anglo-Saxon method (Hansen 1990: 124).

Remember to always write down your sources (i.e., where you have found the information) the first time you use them. Looking up your sources afterwards is very time consuming.

FINAL ADVICE

- Ask yourself: Why is it that most research papers are so visually boring? We live in a society where pictures matter more than ever. Hence, consider creating a unique or creative layout or perhaps an interesting front cover. Remember that you are selling a product.
- Consider making the title of your research paper interesting, such as: 'A corporate brand analysis of an old conservative bank: From folk dance to break dance.' The subtitle refers to the bank's attempt at changing its image; from being old and conservative to being modern and popular.

CHAPTER 17
KEY ELEMENTS IN A GOOD RESEARCH PAPER

Examiners have different preferences; however, most examiners would agree that a good research paper should:

- Have a clear and relevant RQ, and if possible an interesting RQ.
- Have a clear and logical structure throughout the entire research paper. Research papers where the reader continuously has to leaf back and forth are usually not well structured.
- Make sure there is logical coherence between the different chapters.
- Guide the reader through the entire research paper. Almost all experienced examiners put great emphasis on being guided through the research paper. Being guided through a research paper includes ensuring that the structure is clear and that each chapter contains an introduction and a summary.
- Tie data and theory together.
- Only include relevant theories and data.
- Use the data and the theories in the analysis, and include the main pro and cons.
- Be critical, both in relation to your own analysis and conclusions, and in relation to the object of analysis.
- Be objective and open-minded, not black-and-white.
- Account for the validity and reliability of the research paper.
- Include relevant examples to support and enhance the discussion/analysis.
- Last but not least, the spelling—and the language in general—has to be satisfactory.

FINAL ADVICE
- Before handing in your research paper, make sure that the content is

coherent and everything makes sense. This goes for each sentence and chapter, as well as the overall structure. A good strategy is to read your paper at least three times, each time with a new pair of 'reading glasses,' so to speak. The first time, read your paper from an overall structural perspective. The second time, focus on the flow in each chapter and the flow between the chapters. The last time, focus on every single sentence.

- Consider letting somebody who is not familiar with the topic of your research paper read it quickly and see if it makes sense to him or her.
- Note that reading a research paper three times and making any necessary corrections takes more time than most people think. The final proofreading of a sixty-page paper takes at least two to three days.

PART 3
AFTER

This final part of the book is concerned with grading and the issue of oral exams. Initially, the research paper is related to the oral examination. This is followed by a list of some generic elements used by many examiners when grading a research paper.

CHAPTER 18
ORAL EXAMINATIONS

The oral examination normally lasts between twenty and thirty minutes, and the student usually begins with a presentation. The time allocated for these presentations is normally two to five minutes. This is extremely short. Most student presentations end up taking far too much time. To avoid this problem, open with the most important ideas. This is also important in case the examiners have to stop the presentation before it is finished. Grades are based partly on the research paper and partly on the examination, including your presentation. So it is very important to give a good presentation and sell yourself at the examination.

Group members do not automatically get the same grade for the research paper. Usually, at the oral examination every group member–on an individual basis–has to defend the research paper; thus your individual presentation of the research paper at the examination is very important

PREPARING YOUR PRESENTATION

When working in a group it is a good idea to prepare the oral defense (i.e., the individual presentation) of your research paper in your group. However, each person should not end up saying exactly the same things at his or her presentation. Have a brainstorm as a group about the potential topics you could talk about at the examination. This could include the strengths and weaknesses of your research paper or what you could have done differently. After the brainstorming, split up and make individual presentations.

Normally, the first couple of questions at the exam are based on your presentation. This gives you a chance to set the agenda for what will be discussed at the exam. Use this opportunity.

Many students use a PowerPoint presentation. Do not show your presentation on a computer; rather, give a hard copy to the examiners.

Because you have very limited time to sell the project *and* yourself, do not repeat what is in your research paper. The examiners have read the paper. Writing research papers is a constant learning process, so instead you should talk about what could have been improved or done differently (i.e., lessons learned).

Normally I tell my students that if they chose to draw attention to weaknesses, they should focus only on what they could have improved or done differently. Note that some supervisors warn their students against talking too much about the weak aspects, so ask your supervisor what she prefers before preparing your presentation.

GENERIC QUESTIONS AT THE ORAL EXAM

Below are some of the questions normally posed at oral exams:

- To whom would you give your research paper?
- What are the two main recommendations of your research paper?
- Who experiences the problem your RQ deals with?
- What kind of problem is it—economic, political, et cetera?
- Why is 'the problem' a problem?
- What is the definition of a theory?
- What is the difference between a theory and a single empirical survey?
- Can you present some similar cases?
- Why has the organization not done what you recommended in this research paper?
- Explain the structure of the paper very briefly. Why did you structure it the way you did? Could you have done it differently? What are the main strengths and weaknesses of your research paper?
- What would you do differently if you were to solve the same RQ with your present knowledge?
- Can you summarize the main conclusion of your research paper in one sentence?

- Could you have used other theories? Which ones? Why did you not use them?
- Can your conclusions be applied to other organizations? Which ones? How?

Besides these generic questions, examiners often ask about:

- Specific facts and numbers they do not understand.
- Missing sources.
- Sentences they do not understand.
- Contradictions in the research paper.
- Examples of related cases and situations.

FINAL ADVICE

- When asked questions at the exam, think for a couple of seconds and then answer them immediately and directly. After that you can elaborate in more detail on related topics.
- Be specific in your answers.
- Take charge of the discussion. If you can incorporate other relevant theories or cases when answering a question, do so.
- Questions can depend on the examiner's field of interest. So if you know who the examiner is beforehand, check what he/she is working on and prepare accordingly.
- Ask those group members who have just been examined about the questions posed at their exam. You will most likely be asked some of the same questions.
- If you can't make it, fake it. In other words, look confident. Remember, you are the expert on your research paper.

CHAPTER 19
THE GRADING ELEMENTS — THE EXAMINER'S MANUAL

When grading research papers, most examiners use the learning objectives as the main grading criteria, so read the learning objectives in your project manual carefully.

Below are the grading elements that many examiners use when grading a research paper:

- Are the learning objectives fulfilled?
- Is the RQ answered?
- Is the RQ focused and understandable?
- Is the RQ relevant (i.e., is it a real problem)?
- Is the language satisfactory? Are the sentences understandable?
- Is the student independent and critical of his data and findings?
- Is there a table of contents? If so, does it give a good overview?
- Is the structure of the research paper logical?
- Are there logical transitions between the chapters?
- Is the introduction focused and does it lay out the context of the research paper?
- Is the student accounting for his philosophy of science?
- Does the student understand his philosophy of science?
- Is the student presenting good arguments for his methodological choices?
- Are the methodological choices logical?
- Is the student accounting for the consequences of his methodological choices?
- Is the student showing a good understanding of methodology?
- Is there a logical connection between the theories, hypotheses, empirical data, et cetera?
- Has the student found the relevant empirical data?

- Has the student made his own surveys and/or interviews?
- Is the empirical data used in the analysis?
- Are there delimitations and are they relevant?
- Are there many sources and are they sufficiently academic?
- Are there conclusions, and are they relevant and focused?
- Are the sub-questions relevant?
- Are the hypotheses relevant? Are they 'real' hypotheses?
- Are the hypotheses used in the research paper? Does the student draw conclusions regarding the hypotheses?
- Are the chosen theories the right ones?
- Is the student critical of these theories?
- Does the student have a good understanding of the theories?
- Are the theories used in the analysis?
- Does the student use theories that are not in the curriculum?
- Do I have a clear picture of the object of analysis and its main challenges after reading the research paper?
- Are there enough headings and are they relevant?
- Is the research paper repetitive?
- Does the research paper contain a large amount of irrelevant information?
- Is the layout satisfactory? Are there pictures, graphs, or figures?

CHAPTER 20
FEEDBACK AFTER THE EXAMINATION

Writing research papers is a never-ending learning process. Meet with your supervisor after the exam to get feedback that you can use in writing future research papers.

USEFUL BOOKS

Below are some useful books for further reading:

Andersen, I. (2005). *Guide to problem formulation*. For research projects within the social sciences. Frederiksberg: Samfundslitteratur.
Bauer, M.W. and G. Gaskell. (2006). *Qualitative researching with text, image, and sound: A practical handbook*. London: Sage Publications.
Brookes, I. and D. Marshall. (2004). *Good writing guide*. Edinburgh: Chambers.
Bryman, A. (2004). *Social research methods*. Second Edition. New York: Oxford University Press.
Cresswell, J.W. (1998). *Qualitative inquiry and research design: Choosing among five traditions*. London: Sage Publications.
Harboe, T. and R. von Müllen. (2006). *Method of study for international students*. Frederiksberg: Samfundslitteratur.
O'Leary, Z. (2010). *The essential guide to doing your research project*. Second Edition. Los Angeles: Sage publications.
Olsen, P.B. and K. Pedersen. (2005). *Problem-oriented project work: A workbook*. Frederiksberg: Roskilde University Press.
Outwaite, W. and S.P. Turner (eds.). (2007). *The Sage handbook of social science methodology*. Los Angeles: Sage Publications.
Van de Ven, A.H. (2007). *Engaged scholarship: A guide for organizational and social Research*. Oxford: Oxford University Press.
Ragin, C. (1987). *The comparative method*. Berkeley: University of California Press.
Reynolds, P. D. (2007). *A Primer in Theory Construction*. Boston: Pearson.
Silverman, D. (2005). *Doing qualitative research*. London: Sage Publications.
Zinsser, W. (1990). *On writing well*. New York: Harper Collins.

ABOUT THE AUTHOR

Peter Haisler is owner of Sustain Consulting (www.sustainconsulting.dk). He has been teaching methodology and the philosophy of science for more than ten years at CBS, and runs the website www.methology.dk For the past ten years Peter Haisler has also been an external lecturer, supervisor, and censor at the University of Copenhagen, the University of Roskilde, and the Danish Institute for Study Abroad (DIS). As an external lecturer he has been teaching in academic disciplines like corporate social responsibility, corporate governance, global business strategies, and development studies.